TRANSFORMED LIVING

Discover Your Kingdom Assignment

Workbook

Randy R. Butler

Mi Publishing

Copyright © 2024 by Mission Increase.

ISBN: 979-8-9906208-0-3

All rights reserved. No part of this publication may be reproduced, distributed, or transmitted in any form or by any means, including photocopying, recording, or other electronic or mechanical methods, without prior written permission of Mission Increase, except in the case of brief quotations in reviews and certain other noncommercial uses permitted by copyright law.

All scripture quotations are from The Holy Bible, English Standard Version. ESV® Text Edition: 2016. Copyright © 2001 by Crossway Bibles, a publishing ministry of Good News Publishers.

This book follows the pattern of Bible translations like the English Standard Version, the Christian Standard Bible, and the New International Version in not capitalizing pronouns referring to God. Names and titles of God are capitalized.

Cover design and interior layout by Taylor Creative.

Cover photo of Carnegie Hall by Gordon Bell under license by Alamy Stock Photo.

Published by Mission Increase Publishing.

12909 SW 68th Parkway
#455
Portland, OR 97223-8345

For information about ordering copies of the *Transformational Living: Discover Your Kingdom Assignment Workbook*, the *Leader's Guide*, scheduling an in-person workshop with Randy Butler, or accessing the online version of *Transformational Living: Discover Your Kingdom Assignment*, please visit missionincrease.org/transformational-living.

Printed in the United States of America.

TRANSFORMATIONAL LIVING
Discover Your Kingdom Assignment

Workbook

Randy R. Butler

Mi Publishing

TABLE OF CONTENTS

1	Introduction
3	Session One: Are We Ready for Heaven?
6	Session Two: Urgency: Defining Why
9	Session Three: Leverage
12	Session Four: Stewardship
14	Session Five: Time and Head
17	Session Six: Talent and Hands
20	Session Seven: Testimony and Heart
23	Session Eight: Treasure and HHH
26	Session Nine: Principle and Principal
31	Kingdom Business Plan
37	Devotional Guide
71	Spiritual Biographical Sketches
88	Bibliography
93	Acknowledgements

INTRODUCTION

For decades, Paul Harvey held Americans spellbound with his mesmerizing voice and thrilling stories. He was known for taking stories that people had heard before and then telling them, "The rest of the story." People found this captivating because they often suspect there is more to the stories they are being told.

I had this feeling when I watched the History Channel's 2012 epic The Men Who Built America. Millions of people tuned in to watch the fascinating story of how Cornelius Vanderbilt, John D. Rockefeller, Andrew Carnegie, J.P. Morgan, and Henry Ford transformed America from a rural nation of farmers into an economic and industrial powerhouse.

The Men Who Built America offered a portrait of these men that felt incomplete. It portrayed them at their most ruthless and cutthroat without showing that they had motivations other than greed. When you dig deeper into their stories, you find that each of these men had relationships with God, the church, and their pastors. They left behind testimonies to their faith which I found motivating and inspiring.

I set out on a journey to understand the spiritual lives of these great industrialists. Through studying Scripture and their biographies, I started to understand the importance of what I call our "Kingdom Assignment."

Every person who knows Jesus has a unique assignment in this world. It is shaped by our walk with the Lord, through the urgency of the evangelistic task, and in keeping with the gifting that God has given to each of us. As we study the good news of Jesus Christ, the plight of those who haven't believed, the importance of the church, and our spiritual gifting, we come to understand our unique Kingdom Assignment and how God intends for us to fulfill it.

The nine sessions in this workbook are intended to do just that. As we go on this journey together, we will learn about our Kingdom Assignment and how God wants to use you in this world to be a blessing to others.

Are We Ready for Heaven?

Session One

In this session we will introduce you to the basic principles of Transformational Living. We will explore the importance of our Kingdom Assignments and briefly touch on the Kingdom Business Plan you will build at the end of this study.

Before we talk about our individual Kingdom Assignment, we need to discuss the most important question that every person must answer–are we ready for heaven? The answer to that question determines whether or not we are ready for Transformational Living.

Key Truths

> **Key Bible Passage:**
> **Matthew 25:14-30**

Our Aim

What is a Kingdom Assignment?

What will the Kingdom Business Plan help you to do?

What is the focal point in all of this?

Cornelius Vanderbilt gave us _____.

John D. Rockefeller gave us _____.

Andrew Carnegie gave us _____.

J.P. Morgan gave us _____.

Henry Ford gave us _____.

Our assignment is to build _____.

Optimism
When we look at Matthew 25:14-30, what reasons do we have for being optimistic?

Offerings
Where do we see urgency in this passage?

Where do we see leverage in this passage?

How have people around you affirmed that this is your Kingdom Assignment?

Where do we see stewardship in this passage?

In general, are you optimistic or pessimistic about what is happening in the world around us?

Application: (A life of generous, Transformational Living)

Loving God with time: _____.

Loving God with talents: _____.

Loving God with testimony: _____.

Loving God with our treasure: _____.

What evidence do you see that reminds you that God is at work in this world?

Discussion

In our discussion time, we want to discuss where you are now. We will observe and mark how your answers to these questions might change as you work your way through *Transformational Living*.

How often do you pray for friends and family members who are not Christians?

Do you believe that you have a unique Kingdom Assignment? At this stage of your life, what do you think that it is?

What steps can you start taking now to share your faith with them?

In two minutes or less, tell us your testimony of how you came to faith in Christ.

Notes:

Before We Meet Again
Read 1 Thessalonians 4:13-18.

What reasons do we have to be optimistic about the future based on this passage?

What are we supposed to do with the hope that we have?

Session Two

Urgency: Defining Why

Before we embark on any difficult endeavor, it is more important to understand "why" before "how." When you get stuck on "how" without understanding "why," it becomes easy to throw your hands up in frustration. However, when you have defined your "why," you will know why figuring out "how" is important and be better prepared to do it.

In this session, we want to define your "why." We will look at the peril of those who do not know Christ and the difficult times in which we live. Through this, we will come to understand why our Kingdom Assignments are an urgent matter.

Key Truths

> **Key Bible Passage:**
> **Matthew 7:13-14**

How does this passage convince us that our Kingdom Assignments are an urgent matter?

What does this passage say about those who are wrecking their lives through sin?

The call of God on our lives is to share our _____.

God has a Kingdom Assignment for _____ _____.

Few people are living for Jesus in a way that leads to life _____ and _____.

The enemy is _____, the enemy is _____, and the enemy wants to _____ all that God wants to _____.

How did the death of Dr. Butler's son convince him of the urgency of the moment?

What role did his work with the Oregon Youth Authority and as a police chaplain play in demonstrating the importance of urgency to Dr. Butler?

Application
Our message is one of _____!

The urgency of the hour for _____ souls and _____ souls is at a critical junction in world history.

Generous Transformational Living is _____.

Discussion
Read Luke 16:19-31.

How does this passage demonstrate the urgency of us carrying out our Kingdom Assignment?

What trends do we see in our culture that show the urgency of our being witnesses for Christ?

What is your story that showed you the urgency of living for Christ?

How does this present world lull us to sleep and rob us of our urgency?

Who are some people that God has placed in your life that you should generously love this week?

What is one thing we have discussed in this session that you are going to put into practice this week?

Before We Meet Again
Read Ephesians 5:15-16.

How do these verses show us the necessity of urgency?

What practical steps can you take to make the most of the time that you have?

Notes:

What are some areas of your life where you can take what you are already doing and use it for the Kingdom?

Leverage

Session Three

We often miss the ways Jesus can take the ordinary things we take for granted and use them for his glory. God gifted us not just spiritually, but naturally and materially, so that we can make an impact in his kingdom.

In this week's session, we will talk about leverage. In this session, you will come to understand how you can take every aspect of your life and lay it at the feet of Jesus. Then he blesses it, entrusts it to you, and empowers you to use it to make an impact for his kingdom.

Key Truths

> **Key Bible Passage:**
> Luke 24:45-49

The proclamation of the cross of Jesus is our _____ and _____ as witnesses for him.

Why does everything we do each day matter?

What does the Holy Spirit empower us to do?

We need the _____ of the Holy Spirit to _____ through us.

Leverage is defined as things that…

The Lord delights in _____ detail of our lives.

Leverage is putting what we have in the _____ of Jesus through _____ and asking him to bless it.

Application

Embrace the _____ and embrace the _____ of the Holy Spirit in our lives.

Our message is one of _____!!

Generous, Transformational Living is _____.

May God help us to be _____ of Jesus who _____ his church!

Discussion

Think outside of the normal discussion about spiritual gifts. What are natural talents in life, home, and work that you possess?

What needs do you see as you look around your community that you wish someone would do something about?

When you couple your natural talents with the areas of need you see, how can you take these things and put them in the hands of Jesus?

How do you approach your prayer life every day?

What aspects of your normal routine and schedule need to be bathed in prayer so they can be used for God's kingdom?

Think through your plans for tomorrow. What is one thing you can do for God's kingdom tomorrow?

Over the course of a week, how many people do you think you encounter who don't know Jesus?

How can you use the normal things you do each week to engage them with the Gospel?

Before We Meet Again
Read Luke 5:27-32.

Who were the people that Levi invited to meet Jesus after he followed him?

How did Levi probably know the people he invited to the meal?

How does this demonstrate Levi using leverage for the sake of the Kingdom?

Notes:

Session Four

Stewardship

When we hear the word "stewardship," we typically think of money. But we have so many more resources to steward than just our money. The most important areas of stewardship in our lives are not tangible. They don't involve things we can touch.

Today we will learn about how we steward our influence. We influence people through our interactions with them every day. Each interaction is an opportunity for Gospel witness and Gospel impact. After today's session, you will understand how stewardship touches every area of your life.

Key Truths

Key Bible Passage:
Luke 14:16-24

Through our _____ and our _____, we compel people to come to Christ as Savior.

We use our kingdom influence to bring the _____ of _____ to those who desperately need it.

Good things hinder what matters most. We should look for ways to use all of the good things in life for his glory.

What are some good things that hinder what matters most?

God sees value in people that we often don't see. We ought to pray for God to help us see the possibilities and potential for who people can be in him.

Application

We are to be _____ with all people groups in _____ places at _____ times; to this end we _____ what God has given us which leads to effective influence.

Our influence is _____!

Our message is …

Discussion

Tell us about one person who has been the greatest influence on you.

What aspect of this person's influence could you emulate in your interactions with other people?

In what ways do you believe that you are uniquely gifted to serve other people and influence them towards Jesus? Have other people noticed these gifts in you?

Read 1 Peter 4:7-11. What is one way that you can use your spiritual gifting to influence others in the next week?

Read 1 Corinthians 13. Think again about the person who influenced you most. What comes to mind first, their gifts or the way they loved you and spent time with you? What does this tell you about how you are called to use your gifts?

When you compare what you hope people will say at your funeral with how you spend your days now, what changes do you need to make to become the person people described at your funeral?

Before We Meet Again
Read 2 Timothy 4:6-8 and reflect on the funeral question.

Write a short description of what you hope people will say about you. Then take some time and sketch out what changes need to happen in your life to become the person of influence that you hope to be.

Notes:

Session Five

Time and Head

Many people hear about reaching out to people through evangelism, but feel they are too busy to add one more thing to their overflowing plates. Busyness makes us feel guilty because we know how important it is for other people to hear about Jesus.

In this session, you'll learn that living on Jesus' mission does not mean adding another thing to your schedule. Instead, it's about understanding life from an eternal perspective so that everything we do becomes an opportunity to shine the light of Christ.

Key Truths

> **Key Bible Passage:**
> **John 9:4**

Over the next four sessions we will talk about _____, _____, _____, and _____.

God wants us to live our life for him _____.

_____ is the time to do our _____ and give our best to the work.

_____ person counts.
_____ person matters to Jesus.

Why do we have to make the most of our time?

What goal should we set?

How is our day like the days of Noah?

_____ is the time!

_____ is the day of salvation!

What is the invitation at the end of Revelation?

14   **Transformational Living**: Discover Your Kingdom Assignment

All the pieces of the puzzle have to be _____ for it to be a beautiful picture.

Through our Kingdom Assignment, we _____ much more than we give.

Application
Defining what matters most: _____ _____.

We must shift from an _____ perspective to an _____ perspective with both our time and our participation in the Gospel.

_____ matters most!

Discussion
Why do you think we believe that the things we do for God require extra time out of our schedule instead of seeing them as part of what we are already doing?

What opportunities does your current weekly routine give you to interact with other people?

What are some ways that we are tempted to only see our routines from an earthly perspective?

In what ways can you use these opportunities for the kingdom of God?

How does keeping an eternal perspective change the way we think about other people?

Who are people that you encounter on a regular basis who may not know Jesus?

What are some ways that you can begin to bless one person every day?

Before We Meet Again
Read James 2:1-6.

Who are people you encounter in your routines that you tend to overlook based only on their appearance or social class?

Transformational Living: Discover Your Kingdom Assignment

How can thinking about these people from an eternal perspective change the way you interact with them?

Notes:

What are some of the ways you might seek to bless the people on your list?

Talent and Hands

Session Six

Every Christian is a walking miracle. We experienced a supernatural change of heart through faith in Jesus Christ that no human power could manufacture. God works these miracles every day and he does them through people like you and me.

Today you'll discover that as the Holy Spirit works through you, the ordinary things you do every day become miracles. Through his power, everything we do in Jesus' name has the power to change lives for eternity.

Key Truths

> **Key Bible Passage:**
> **Acts 1:8**

What do we mean by a miracle?

To God _____!

Every God-given talent is for this purpose:

Power to witness: We are his _____, his _____, and his _____ extended to people who are hurting and lonely and lost.

What two ordinary things would make a big difference in our witness?

God gives us the power to _____, to _____, to _____, and then to _____.

Everyone has _____.

_____ is love and love is _____.

What was miraculous about Zacchaeus's conversion?

Transformational Living: Discover Your Kingdom Assignment

Application
Be a _____.

With our _____ and active engagement, we have an opportunity to be a _____ in someone's life.

Discussion
In what ways have you seen God miraculously work in the ordinary routines of your life?

What would it look like for you to glorify God in the ordinary ways that you live your life right now?

Did you agree that kindness and a smile could make a big difference in other's lives? Why, or why not?

Where are the areas in your community where people are unloved and uncared for?

What are some practical ways that you could help meet the needs of those people in your community?

Think about the story of Zaccheus and the story of the woman in Luke 7. What do their stories have in common?

What do the stories of these two people tell us about living every day for Jesus?

As we have talked in this session, have people come to your mind that you need to pray for and reach out to? What steps can you begin to take to do that?

Before We Meet Again
Write out the testimony of how you came to Christ. Include your life before you knew Christ, how you came to know Christ, and how Christ has changed your life.

Notes:

Practice saying your testimony out loud until you can tell your story in around three minutes.

Session Seven

Testimony and Heart

In last session's homework, we asked you to write out your testimony. As you read over your testimony, you will probably see the names of people who loved you and told you about Jesus. We have the privilege of playing the same role in other people's stories as they come to know Jesus too.

This session focuses on your testimony. Every Christian has a testimony and every Christian's testimony is a miracle. Through this session, you will see how your experience of Jesus and your time with Jesus can make a real difference in the lives of people around you.

Key Truths

> **Key Bible Passage:**
> Acts 4:13-20

What is Transformational Living all about?

Big _____, big _____, big _____.

What happens as we spend more time with Jesus?

What did the Apostles say they could not stop doing?

We serve a powerful God and he works through _____.

What we need in our testimony is for it to be _____, _____, _____, and _____.

The more _____ we spend with Jesus the more we can _____ about him.

When we spend more time with Jesus....

We have an _____ to make Jesus our highest _____.

After we have given Jesus all of _____, shouldn't our prayer be, "Jesus, we want all of _____"?

Transformational Living is....

Application
Be an _____ for Jesus.

Our _____ hinges on _____ with Jesus.

Our testimony becomes _____ and we own a share in the _____ and the empty tomb.

Discussion
What is your routine for spending time with God through Bible reading and prayer?

Do you find your Bible study routine to be fulfilling or does it need some adjustments?

What are some ways you have seen the goodness of God recently?

How can your experience of God's goodness be encouraging to other people?

Why does it encourage you to know that Jesus died for you?

Why does it encourage you to know that Jesus rose from the dead?

When you consider how the cross and empty tomb have encouraged you, who is someone you know that could use that same encouragement?

Before We Meet Again
Read 2 Corinthians 5:16-21.

What happens to every person who is in Christ?

What is the message that we have as ambassadors for Christ?

Notes:

Treasure and HHH

Session Eight

We think about money every day of our lives. We stress over how little we have, how much more we need, and how we are going to make what we have stretch until we get more. Unfortunately, we tend to spend less time thinking about our money from a biblical and spiritual perspective.

In this session, we want to think about how God intends for us to use our earthly treasures for his kingdom. We will discover together that God has given us enough to be generous towards others. In so doing, we won't just be a blessing to others, but a blessing to God as well.

Key Truths

> **Key Bible Passage:**
> **1 Timothy 6:17-19**

Treasure follows our _____.

Be rich in good works through _____ toward _____.

Where does Matthew 6:19-21 say we should store up our treasure?

What we have in Jesus is our _____.

His call upon our lives is…

The Kingdom Assignment is…

What flows from there is _____.

Money becomes a blessing when we give him…

Part of our Kingdom Assignment is to experience the _____ of God.

Application

Be a _____ to God and others.

This is how we utilize our _____, _____, _____, and _____.

Our highest aim: _____ God!

Transformational Living: Discover Your Kingdom Assignment

Discussion

What was the first job that you had where you earned a paycheck? What were your emotions when payday came?

Who was someone in your life who modeled sacrificial giving? What did you learn from them?

What are some reasons that we are tempted to be stingy with our giving?

If God is our Father, how should that affect the way we think about how he provides for us?

If our true treasure is in heaven, how should that change the way we view our earthly treasure?

What lifestyle changes would you need to make to free up more money to show generosity?

What role should our prayer lives play in our generosity?

What steps can you take this week to be more generous with what God has given you?

Before We Meet Again
Read 2 Corinthians 8:9.

What were the riches that Jesus gave up when he came to earth?

How should Jesus' generosity towards us change the way we think about our own generosity?

Notes:

Session Nine

Principle and Principal

As we come to the end of these nine sessions, we want to talk about a concept that will tie everything together, that is understanding the difference between principle *and* principal. *You will see that principle will help you define what is important in life and principal is one of the tools to help you get through life.*

After this session, you can prepare to fill out your Kingdom Business Plan and start working through the 30-Days Toward Your Kingdom Business Plan. Our prayer is that as you use these tools, you will see that Transformational Living is not a nine-week study, but a lens through which you view the life that God has given to you.

Key Truths

> **Key Bible Passage:**
> **Matthew 6:25-34**

All these things are the things we _____ about, _____ about, and really believe that we need for _____.

The question is, do we really _____?

Tomorrow has enough...

A *principal* is a _____ of _____.

When we are governed by the _____ rather than the _____, we get the _____ of _____ right.

Integrity is _____ we do and _____ we are when no one is watching or when everyone is watching.

Seek _____ and _____ the kingdom of God.

We cannot give to others...

Principle has to do with the _____ of _____.

_____ on today. _____ _____, as many as we possibly can!

Transformational Living: Discover Your Kingdom Assignment

What is our Kingdom Assignment? It is _____.

God has a _____ for your life.

He has given us an _____ that no one can _____.

Application
The difference between _____ and _____ can determine the eternal destiny of many souls.

This passage teaches us what to _____.

People need...

Discussion
What is the most difficult decision that you have ever made?

How did you seek the Lord through that decision?

In the end, how did you know which decision to make?

What do you think will be different about your life going forward after walking through this study?

Through this study, how has your understanding of your Kingdom Assignment changed?

What excites you the most about thinking through your Kingdom Business Plan?

Who are some people who are going to hold you accountable on finishing your Kingdom Business Plan?

Notes:

A Word from the Author

Thank you so much for your commitment to *Transformational Living: Discover Your Kingdom Assignment.* The nine-session study you just completed was my part of this tool. Finding the heart of God for your Kingdom Business Plan is your part—yours and the Holy Spirit's.

In the next two sections you will seek God and his will for direction in your own life. You will reflect on the videos you watched, the material you read, the questions you answered, and the notes you took. You will pray and reflect on where God has you right now, what his Kingdom Business Plan is for your life, and write down the steps needed to pursue it.

Beginning on page 32, you will start fleshing out your Kingdom Business Plan. You will return to these pages over and over as you work through the 30-Days Toward a Kingdom Business Plan Devotional Guide (pages 39-68).

The section entitled 30-Days Toward a Kingdom Business Plan is where you meditate on and record your daily interaction with God as it relates to your Kingdom Business Plan. Each day, review the four "What is" questions, journaling your thoughts, insights, and new directions. As parts 1–9 start becoming clear, write and rewrite your thoughts in the space provided until you can finalize them.

Lastly, remember Paul's prayer in Ephesians 3:14–21:

> For this reason I bow my knees before the Father, from whom every family in heaven and on earth is named, that according to the riches of his glory he may grant you to be strengthened with power through his Spirit in your inner being, so that Christ may dwell in your hearts through faith—that you, being rooted and grounded in love, may have strength to comprehend with all the saints what is the breadth and length and height and depth, and to know the love of Christ that surpasses knowledge, that you may be filled with all the fullness of God. Now to him who is able to do far more abundantly than all that we ask or think, according to the power at work within us, to him be glory in the church and in Christ Jesus throughout all generations, forever and ever. Amen. (ESV)

In Christ,

Randy

TRANSFORMATIONAL LIVING

Discover Your Kingdom Assignment

Kingdom Business Plan

Kingdom Business Plan:
Fleshing Out Your Kingdom Assignment

"Then he said to me, 'This is the word of the Lord to Zerubbabel: Not by might, nor by power, but by my Spirit,' says the Lord of hosts." (Zechariah 4:6)

"He has told you, O man, what is good; and what does the Lord require of you but to do justice, to love kindness, and to walk humbly with your God?" (Micah 6:8)

"But you will receive power when the Holy Spirit has come upon you, and you will be my witnesses in Jerusalem and in all Judea and Samaria, and to the end of the earth." (Acts 1:8)

What is my call from God?
Scripture:

What is my assignment from God?
Scripture:

What is my mission from God?
Scripture:

What is my mandate from God?
Scripture:

1. Mission Statement. Start with "My mission is…" and answer the question, "What does God want me to do?"

Scripture:

2. Vision Statement. Start with "My vision is…" and answer the question, "Where does God want me to go?"

Scripture:

3. Aim Statement. Start with "My aim is…" and answer the question, "What do I hope to achieve?

Scripture:

4. Objective Statement: Start with "My objective is…" and answer the question, "What are the measurable outcomes?"

Scripture:

5. Scope: Outline the work needed to develop your product.

Scripture:

6. What is my cause?

Scripture:

7. What are my goals?

Scripture:

8. What is my "why?"

Scripture:

9. What are my next steps?

Scripture:

PRAY, PRAY, PRAY

TRANSFORMATIONAL LIVING

Discover Your Kingdom Assignment

Devotional Guide

Follow these steps for a more productive daily devotional time:

- Set aside 20-30 minutes for your study.
- Go to a distraction-free place.
- If you listen to music, choose instrumental pieces.
- Begin with prayer for God's guidance.
- Read through the daily scripture slowly, noting anything that directly addresses your Kingdom Business Plan.
- Complete each of the four sections including a written prayer.
- Review Fleshing Our Your Kingdom Business Plan and write down any new thoughts.

Day One

Transformational Living is letting God be God and me be me.

TODAY'S FOCUS
Exodus 3 & 4
Head - God is the great I AM! I am not.
Heart - Trust in God no matter what.
Hands - Please use me and please help me as you use me.

Scriptures & HHH: _____

My assignment this week includes: _____

My Kingdom Business Plan progress: _____

My prayer: _____

Day Two

Transformational Living is bringing Jesus into discussions; bragging on Jesus; returning to Jesus in conversation.

TODAY'S FOCUS
John 10:10
Head - The thief is never my friend.
Heart - Jesus wants my heart to be full of life in him.
Hands - Touch someone because Jesus has touched me.

Scriptures & HHH: _____

My assignment this week includes: _____

My Kingdom Business Plan progress: _____

My prayer: _____

Day Three
Transformational Living is the full release of anxiety, fear, stress, doubt, and worry.

TODAY'S FOCUS
Matthew 6:25-34
Head - Nearly everything I worry about does not happen.
Heart - I have a blessed assurance that everything is ok with Jesus.
Hands - I need to demonstrate faith and not live in fear.

Scriptures & HHH: _____

My assignment this week includes: _____

My Kingdom Business Plan progress: _____

My prayer: _____

Transformational Living: Discover Your Kingdom Assignment

Day Four

Transformational Living has visible, measurable, spiritual results.

TODAY'S FOCUS
Matthew 28:18-20
Head - Remember daily the teachings of Jesus.
Heart - God, please give me a bold heart.
Hands - Go do something for God.

Scriptures & HHH: _____

My assignment this week includes: _____

My Kingdom Business Plan progress: _____

My prayer: _____

Day Five

Transformational Living is combining in harmony and in unity, my head (how I manage my earthly time), my heart (how I stay on fire for God), and my hands (how I touch others in the name of Jesus).

TODAY'S FOCUS
Acts 1:8
Head - Be faithful.
Heart - Be filled.
Hands - Be fruitful.

Scriptures & HHH: _____

My assignment this week includes: _____

My Kingdom Business Plan progress: _____

My prayer: _____

Transformational Living: Discover Your Kingdom Assignment

Day Six

Transformational Living is *the peace of God beyond human comprehension* **(Philippians 4:7).**

TODAY'S FOCUS
Philippians 4:7
Head - Peace in my brain.
Heart - Peace in my heart.
Hands - Freedom to help hurting people.

Scriptures & HHH: _____

My assignment this week includes: _____

My Kingdom Business Plan progress: _____

My prayer: _____

Day Seven
Transformational Living is intimacy with God.

TODAY'S FOCUS
Deuteronomy 6:4-9
Head - Mind love.
Heart - Heart and soul love.
Hands - Love in action.

Scriptures & HHH: _____

My assignment this week includes: _____

My Kingdom Business Plan progress: _____

My prayer: _____

Day Eight
Transformational Living is a covenant, not a contract.

TODAY'S FOCUS
Ezekiel 36:26-27
Head - I knew something was wrong and only Jesus could help me.
Heart - A brand new heart.
Hands - A much better way to live life.

Scriptures & HHH: _____
_____
_____
_____
_____
_____
_____

My assignment this week includes: _____
_____
_____
_____
_____
_____
_____

My Kingdom Business Plan progress: _____
_____
_____
_____
_____
_____
_____

My prayer: _____
_____
_____
_____
_____
_____
_____

Day Nine
Transformational Living is awesome.

TODAY'S FOCUS
Genesis 1
Head - My finite mind cannot grasp the depth of Creation; yet I fully believe it.
Heart - My heart completely embraces Creation.
Hands - My life reflects his image in Creation, which leads to human flourishing.

Scriptures & HHH: _____

My assignment this week includes: _____

My Kingdom Business Plan progress: _____

My prayer: _____

Day Ten

Transformational Living is relationship not religion.

TODAY'S FOCUS
John 3:16-17
Head - I know God loves me.
Heart - I am so thankful Jesus died for me.
Hands - I want to tell others about Jesus, his cross, and his love for them.

Scriptures & HHH: _____

My assignment this week includes: _____

My Kingdom Business Plan progress: _____

My prayer: _____

Day Eleven

Transformational Living is a relationship with Christ which is more than a relationship with Christianity.

TODAY'S FOCUS
Matthew 11:28-30
Head - Even when walking closely with God, life can be challenging.
Heart - My heart and my soul need rest regularly.
Hands - I must be constantly moving towards God.

Scriptures & HHH: _____

My assignment this week includes: _____

My Kingdom Business Plan progress: _____

My prayer: _____

Day Twelve
Transformational Living is a follower of Christ who helps others follow Christ.

TODAY'S FOCUS
Matthew 4:19
Head - Sometimes the things of God do not make sense, but they always *work together for good*.
Heart - Lord, please give me a heart for all people.
Hands - Go where I believe Jesus is going to be.

Scriptures & HHH: _____
_____
_____
_____
_____
_____
_____
_____

My assignment this week includes: _____
_____
_____
_____
_____
_____
_____
_____

My Kingdom Business Plan progress: _____
_____
_____
_____
_____
_____
_____
_____

My prayer: _____
_____
_____
_____
_____
_____
_____
_____

Day Thirteen

Transformational Living is continually giving God all of me and continually seeking more of him.

TODAY'S FOCUS
2 Chronicles 16:9
Head - Think about God as much as possible.
Heart - All my heart, all the time, always given to Jesus.
Hands - All my life, all the time, always given to Jesus.

Scriptures & HHH: _____

My assignment this week includes: _____

My Kingdom Business Plan progress: _____

My prayer: _____

Day Fourteen

Transformational Living is a deep well of fresh water in troubled times.

TODAY'S FOCUS
John 4
Head - Think pure thoughts.
Heart - Purity matters.
Hands - Stay clean and close to God.

Scriptures & HHH: _____
_____
_____
_____
_____
_____
_____

My assignment this week includes: _____
_____
_____
_____
_____
_____
_____

My Kingdom Business Plan progress: _____
_____
_____
_____
_____
_____
_____

My prayer: _____
_____
_____
_____
_____
_____
_____

Day Fifteen

Transformational Living is *Christ in you the hope of glory* (Colossians 1:27).

TODAY'S FOCUS
Colossians 1:22
Head - Hope fuels my thought life.
Heart - Christ is always in my heart and that gets me through tough times.
Hands - There is an urgency I need to remember with my assignment to God.

Scriptures & HHH: _____

My assignment this week includes: _____

My Kingdom Business Plan progress: _____

My prayer: _____

Day Sixteen
Transformational Living is wholeness, holiness, and happiness.

TODAY'S FOCUS
Acts 2:42-47
Head - I know Jesus, the Way.
Heart - I love Jesus and his way to love others.
Hands - I know the way to live because I know the Way, who is Jesus.

Scriptures & HHH: _____

My assignment this week includes: _____

My Kingdom Business Plan progress: _____

My prayer: _____

Day Seventeen
Transformational Living is God forming the best in me.

TODAY'S FOCUS
Romans 6:1-11
Head - My life is in Christ, and I must never forget this eternal truth.
Heart - My heart is united with the heart of Christ.
Hands - Don't sin.

Scriptures & HHH: _____

My assignment this week includes: _____

My Kingdom Business Plan progress: _____

My prayer: _____

Day Eighteen

Transformational Living is leverage in relationships, leverage in assignments, leverage in influence.

TODAY'S FOCUS
Matthew 6:9-13
Head - Prayer is stronger than any power on earth.
Heart - *Our Father*, it is a heart relationship.
Hands - Fast and pray.

Scriptures & HHH: _____

My assignment this week includes: _____

My Kingdom Business Plan progress: _____

My prayer: _____

Day Nineteen
Transformational Living is intentionally stewarding Jesus.

TODAY'S FOCUS
1 Corinthians 11:23-28
Head - God, check the motives of my thinking.
Heart - God, check the motives of my heart.
Hands - God, check the motives of my actions.

Scriptures & HHH: _____

My assignment this week includes: _____

My Kingdom Business Plan progress: _____

My prayer: _____

Day Twenty

Transformational Living is a God vision not a man vision.

TODAY'S FOCUS
John 4:35
Head - Big God.
Heart - Big faith.
Hands - Big results.

Scriptures & HHH: _____

My assignment this week includes: _____

My Kingdom Business Plan progress: _____

My prayer: _____

Day Twenty-One
Transformational Living is kingdom living.

TODAY'S FOCUS
Matthew 6:33
Head - Seek God.
Heart - Live for God.
Hands - Work with God for his Kingdom.

Scriptures & HHH: _____

My assignment this week includes: _____

My Kingdom Business Plan progress: _____

My prayer: _____

Transformational Living: Discover Your Kingdom Assignment

Day Twenty-Two
Transformational Living is freedom.

TODAY'S FOCUS
2 Corinthians 3:17
Head - Freedom from all bondage.
Heart - Spirit led.
Hands - Spirit controlled.

Scriptures & HHH: _____

My assignment this week includes: _____

My Kingdom Business Plan progress: _____

My prayer: _____

Day Twenty-Three

Transformational Living is the fulfillment of the fruit of the Spirit.

TODAY'S FOCUS
Galatians 5:22-23
Head - Lord, help me when I lack the fruit of the Spirit.
Heart - Full surrender.
Hands - Behavior matters greatly.

Scriptures & HHH:

My assignment this week includes:

My Kingdom Business Plan progress:

My prayer:

Day Twenty-Four

Transformational Living is Christ magnified and glorified.

TODAY'S FOCUS
1 Chronicles 29:11-13
Head - God is omnipotent, and all glory goes to him alone.
Heart - I exalt Thee. I exalt Thee.
Hands - My life is in your hands.

Scriptures & HHH: _____

My assignment this week includes: _____

My Kingdom Business Plan progress: _____

My prayer: _____

Day Twenty-Five
Transformational Living is not from, not for, but with.

TODAY'S FOCUS
Philippians 4:13
Head - *I can.*
Heart - *Through Christ.*
Hands - God gives me strength.

Scriptures & HHH: _____

My assignment this week includes: _____

My Kingdom Business Plan progress: _____

My prayer: _____

Day Twenty-Six
Transformational Living is abundant living.

TODAY'S FOCUS
Psalm 23
Head - *The Lord is my Shepherd* meeting all my needs.
Heart - *He restores my soul.*
Hands - *Paths of righteousness* are always the will of God.

Scriptures & HHH: _____

My assignment this week includes: _____

My Kingdom Business Plan progress: _____

My prayer: _____

Day Twenty-Seven
Transformational Living is evidence that Jesus is alive.

TODAY'S FOCUS
Matthew 28:1-10; Mark 16:1-8; Luke 24:1-12; John 21:1-18
Head – Many eyewitnesses.
Heart – The Holy Spirit speaks to my heart.
Hands – My testimony is from the Lord.

Scriptures & HHH: _____

My assignment this week includes: _____

My Kingdom Business Plan progress: _____

My prayer: _____

Day Twenty-Eight
Transformational Living is being in the perfect will of God.

TODAY'S FOCUS
Romans 12:2
Head – *Do not conform* but seek mind renewal in him.
Heart – *Be transformed* all the time.
Hands – Do the will of God every day.

Scriptures & HHH: _____

My assignment this week includes: _____

My Kingdom Business Plan progress: _____

My prayer: _____

Day Twenty-Nine

Transformational Living is being a living sacrifice.

TODAY'S FOCUS
Romans 12:1
Head – Figure out how to be a *living sacrifice*.
Heart – Holy, holy, holy.
Hands – *Reasonable service* God's way.

Scriptures & HHH: _____

My assignment this week includes: _____

My Kingdom Business Plan progress: _____

My prayer: _____

Transformational Living: Discover Your Kingdom Assignment

Day Thirty

Transformational Living is being a servant.

TODAY'S FOCUS
Philippians 2:1-11
Head – One mind-*the mind of Christ.*
Heart – *Humility as much as possible.*
Hands – Obedience every day.

Scriptures & HHH: _____

My assignment this week includes: _____

My Kingdom Business Plan progress: _____

My prayer: _____

TRANSFORMATIONAL LIVING
Discover Your Kingdom Assignment
Spiritual Biographical Sketches

Spiritual Biographical Sketches of Vanderbilt, Rockefeller, Carnegie, Morgan, and Ford

The citations that follow show evidence of the influence of Christianity on the lives of Vanderbilt, Rockefeller, Carnegie, Morgan and Ford. Furthermore, the reader will discover the profound impact their pastors (and the church) had on their lives. The exception is Vanderbilt, who converted to Christianity late in life. Even so, he bought a church for his pastor.

For context:
- Charles Deems was pastor and personal advisor to Vanderbilt.
- Fred Gates was a pastor and personal advisor to Rockefeller.
- Henry Sloan Coffin was pastor to Carnegie.
- William S. Rainsford was pastor to Morgan.
- Samuel Marquis was pastor and advisor and employee to Ford.

Furthermore, the following women played significant roles in their homes and marriages and influenced spirituality and generosity of their husbands:

- Frank Howard was Vanderbilt's second wife.
- Laura "Cettie" Spelman was Rockefeller's wife.
- Louise Whitfield was Carnegie's wife.
- Francis Louise Tracy was Morgan's second wife.
- Clara Bryant was Ford's wife.

The author has chosen to present the following evidence book by book, not necessarily in sequential order or in order of importance. The reader is invited to look at the evidence in its total sum and discover the impact God had on these industrialists' lives. The Bible and their faith in God helped to shape their business and philanthropy philosophies, their economic theologies, and their decision-making processes.

With over one hundred volumes listed in the *Transformational Living: Discover Your Kingdom Assignment* bibliography, the author is aware of how these five men have been painted throughout history. It is his privilege to share their faith in God. Are they perfect? No! They are human beings who were ordained by God to change the world, and in so doing, they accumulated vast sums of money, much of which was deployed into the Kingdom during their lifetime and beyond.

Since 2012, the author has been on a journey with these five industrialists. To his joy and surprise, they intersected with his own Christianity. They have inspired, encouraged, and challenged the author. This project is a fulfillment of the author's Kingdom Assignment from God, for such a time as this.

Lessons emerged inspired by the author's extensive research of these five great industrialists, including an emphasis on urgency, leverage, and stewardship (time, talent, testimony and treasure). The author gleaned wisdom on the removal of burdens and restoration of blessings.

Finding gold nuggets does not come easily. They take much effort to uncover and secure. The *Transformational Living:*

Discover Your Kingdom Assignment content is based partially on the lives of these industrialists and is the result of over a decade of study by the author.

Absorb and enjoy,
    be blessed,
        be changed,
            be encouraged,
                be inspired,
                      be renewed,
                          be different,
                              be stronger,
by the evidence recorded in the citations below, much of which was unknown by the masses of the last century.

The author has been a licensed minister since 1980 and pastored churches most of those years. He conducted many funerals, memorial services, and celebration of life services. Never has the author heard negative remarks shared about the life of the person being memorialized. Yet, for these five: Vanderbilt, Rockefeller, Carnegie, Morgan, and Ford, much criticism was leveled at them when they were alive and in some cases, even sharper criticism after their death.

Imagine for a moment:
    You, the reader, just entered a memorial service in a local church. You received a bulletin, signed the guest book, and have taken a seat in the sanctuary. The service is about to begin. You are sitting in a church built with supplies that came via railroads, thanks to Vanderbilt. Your car is fueled, compliments of Rockefeller. You may have safely driven over a steel bridge on the way to the church, courtesy of Carnegie. The reader had the financial means to attend, partially thanks to Morgan. Finally, you drove your car to the memorial service, in part, thanks to Ford. Our lives have already intersected with these five great industrialists.

As the late Paul Harvey used to say on his radio broadcasts…

"And now, the rest of the story…"

On the pages to follow, explore the influence of Christianity on the lives of these five great American industrialists.

Cornelius "Commodore" Vanderbilt (1794-1877)

Commodore Vanderbilt: An Epic of American Achievement
by Arthur D. Howden Smith

She never got him to church, but she did succeed in introducing a clergyman as a regular visitor to the household and ultimately made this person, Rev. Charles F. Deems, his intimate advisor. Her greatest achievement, probably, was in persuading him to reverse his dictum against charity. Dr. Deems is usually credited with inducing him to make this departure from his lifelong rule, but Mrs. Frank must have been the silent mainspring of the kindly conspiracy. Surely, Corneel would never have given $50,000 to buy the Church of the Strangers for Deems without suggestions having been made in the home circle. And while it is true that Deems brought him in touch with Southern clergymen who were agitating the educational needs of their war-torn region, his wife's descriptions of the South's sufferings were certainly a factor in carrying him to the point of giving $1,000,000 to found and endow Vanderbilt University. However, you regard it, Mrs. Frank was a force to be reckoned with. If she lacked the shrewd and pungent personality of Phoebe Hand and the self-effacing devotion of Sophia, she nursed and tended a crotchety, fierce, old man, who was dreaded in his periodic rages by all who must approach him, and gentled him into paths of humility he had never trod before. She deserves her place in the small gallery of women who molded his character. (p. 304-305)

Memorial tablet erected to the late Commodore Vanderbilt in the Church of the Strangers, New York City...Erected to the Glory of God and in memory of Cornelius Vanderbilt by the Church of the Strangers... He was worthy for he hath built us a synagogue. (p. 309)

Thinking on the subject, and with his young wife and Dr. Deems ready to spur his inward scrutiny, he became mildly religious. He didn't go to church, as did eighty percent of Americans in that churchgoing era, but he liked to hear and participate in religious discussion at home. (p. 318)

Of books he knew nothing at all, except for the dog-eared copy of Pilgrim's Progress which his wife had given him. (p. 319)

Religion, as his wife and Dr. Deems taught it, had weaned him finally from spiritualism. (p. 328)

He was glad to have lived in such interesting times. He noticed, in the excitement of the holidays, that the Shadow seemed to have lifted slightly, and for a day or so he felt lighthearted; but then he realized his foolishness, and chuckled, in his quiet, grim way, to himself. Joke was on him, b' God. Hold on, he might cuss. Jesus was his friend, Deems said. Frank believed it, too. Call on Jesus, they said. (p. 329)

On January 3, he was so well that he sat up, and talked to his callers, but after he returned to bed that night, he felt strange. Frank came hastily, Billy and the gals and their husbands. Linsley was there, and three or four more doctors. Deems entered towards morning, quiet-footed, deferential. The clergyman talked to Mrs. Crawford, Frank's mother (Frank was the wife of Vanderbilt) standing by the bed foot, and Corneel beckoned to them weakly. "Sing," he whispered, "hymn." Mrs. Crawford raised her voice, and one by one the rest joined in, "Come ye sinners, poor and needy," they sang and when he signed for more, "Nearer My God to Thee" and "Show Pity, Lord." He asked for Dr. Deems to pray, listening avidly as the words fell from the clergyman's lips. "That's a good prayer," he murmured. His fingers groped out, and fastened upon Deems's hand. "I'll never give up trust in Jesus," he quavered. "How could I let that go?" The Shadow settled over him like a blanket, cool, soothing, pleasantly restful. Rest, that was what he needed. (p. 330-331)

John D. Rockefeller (1839-1937)

Toward the Well-Being of Mankind
by Robert Shaplen

Gates, a fervid evangelist, who, as Fosdick adds, "could never be anything but candid and forthright" is reported to have thundered at the elder Rockefeller, "your fortune is rolling up, rolling up like an avalanche. You must keep up with it! You must distribute it faster than it grows! If you do not, it will crush you and your children and your children's children!" (p. 5)

Random Reminiscences of Men and Events
by John D. Rockefeller

The education of children in my early days may have been straightlaced, yet I have always been thankful that the custom was quite general to teach young people to give systematically of money that they themselves have earned. (p. 146)

Up to the present time no scheme has yet presented itself which seems to afford a better method of handling capital than that of individual ownership. We might put our money into the Treasury of the Nation and of the various states, but we do not find any promise in the National or state legislatures, viewed from the experiences of the past, that the funds would be expended for the general weal more effectively than under the present methods, nor do we find any of the schemes of socialism a promise that wealth would be more wisely administered for the general good. (p. 159-160)

If a combination to do business is effective in saving waste and in getting better results, why is not combination far more important in philanthropic work? The general idea of a cooperation in giving for education, I have felt, scored a real step in advance when Mr. Andrew Carnegie consented to become a member of the General Education Board. For in accepting a position in this directorate he has, it seems to me, stamped with his approval this vital principle of cooperation in aiding the education institutions of our country. (p. 165)

Doctors, clergymen, lawyers, as well as many highgrade men of affairs, are devoting their best and most unselfish efforts to some of the plans we are all trying to work out. (p. 167)

Dear Father/Dear Son
by Joseph W. Ernst

Sept 24, 1893

Dear Father,
Our class is the largest which had ever entered college, and numbers about 175. Grandmother will be interested to know that there are three colored men in the class. We had a class prayer meeting the other afternoon, and you would have been much pleased with the spirit exhibited. Before the meeting was over, all the men from the three other class prayer meetings came in a single file singing "Blessed be the tie that binds," and while they sang they walked through one line of seats and then another, and every one of them shook hands with every man in our class. Then they all stood around, and one of them prayed, and then said a few words about the responsibility resting on each one of us, and the amount of good that a band of fellows could do if they would stand together. (p. 11)

January 18, 1909

Dear Son,
I thank you a thousand times for the fur coat

and cap and mittens. I did not feel that I could afford such luxuries and am grateful for a son who is able to buy them for me. Be assured they are much appreciated. (p. 30)

March 17, 1909

Dear Father,
The monetary value of these gifts is of course tremendous, running into a number of millions of dollars and I do not for a moment underestimate its proportions. But to me their greatest worth lies in the fact that they give evidence of your deep confidence in me and in my earnest purpose under God to use my life and my opportunities and my possessions as my Heavenly Father may direct and my earthly parents would approve. This confidence I prize above all else, and to merit such approval do I daily strive. (p. 35)

February 11, 1919

Dear Father,
May the God who has led you so wonderfully during all of these years of your life, whom you have served so faithfully and untiringly, lead me in the same path of duty and of service and help me to carry on worthily the works for mankind which with marvelous provision you have so solidly and wisely established. (p. 90)

By 1922 Senior had given Junior over $465 million. The large gifts were made between 1916 and 1922... (p. 225)

John D. Rockefeller and his son John D. Rockefeller Jr., shared in the adventure once described by Senior as an effort toward making a better world. This is the legacy of their understanding of their stewardship. (p. 229)

John D. Rockefeller: The Cleveland Years by Grace Goulder

Remembering His Bible's warnings about pride and its dangers, he declared he seldom put his head "upon the pillow at night without speaking a few words to myself." What he termed, "these intimate conversations with myself" came to be more or less habitual throughout his life. He was thus enabled "to stand prosperity" and was saved from getting "puffed up" as he put it. His religion was a practical religion as befitted to a practical man. He used his Bible freely like a tool. (p. 45)

Perhaps it was at anti-slavery meetings that Rockefeller renewed his acquaintance with Laura Celestia Spelman- "Cettie" to her classmates, and "Cettie" to John. The Spelmans were ardent abolitionists. Rockefeller, too, it would seem was driven early into the crusade judging from his gifts to negro causes. (p. 62)

Later as Mrs. John D. Rockefeller, she took no part in her husband's business affairs. As appeals for help mounted, Rockefeller's giving reflected his wife's point of view as much as his own. (p. 66)

Always committed to go to Sunday morning and evening Church. (p. 71)

From his marriage on, John D. made his wife a partner in his giving. (p. 104)

He was no novice in the role of chairman, for he had learned the art as a teen-ager when appointed head of the Erie Street Church's board of trustees, all older than he. Except for Colonel Payne, the Standard's new directors were also his seniors. (p. 115)

With these events swirling about him, his church was never neglected. He took his place as a superintendent of the Sunday

School at the Euclid Avenue Baptist Church and made notes about the sermon for Laura if she was unable to attend. (p. 120)
John and Laura Rockefeller seemed more concerned with their children's spiritual than with their physical wellbeing. (p. 123)

The Rockefellers' purpose this time was to see their daughter, Mrs. Charles Strong (Bessie) who was ill, suffering from a nervous malady in which she was obsessed with the fear of dying in poverty. (p. 201)

Memoirs
by David Rockefeller

"...to promote the wellbeing of mankind throughout the world." (p. 210)

Standard Oil made Grandfather rich, possibly "the richest man in America." He was also, for much of his life, one of the most hated. The tabloid press attacked Standard's business practices and accused it of crimes- including murder…

Grandfather was the target of Progressives, Populists, Socialists, and other discontented with the new American capitalist order… Robert La Follette, the powerful governor of Wisconsin, called him the "greatest criminal of his age…"

Ida Tarbell, who through her writings probably did more than anyone to establish the image of Grandfather as greedy and rapacious "robber baron," wrote, "There is little doubt that Mr. Rockefeller's chief reason for playing golf is that he may live longer to make more money." (p. 5)

In my view it was my Grandfather's deep religious faith that gave him his placid self-assurance in the face of personal attacks, and supreme confidence that enabled him to consolidate the American oil industry. He was a devout Christian who lived by the strict tenets of his Baptist faith. His faith "explained" the world around him on his way through it and provided him with a liberating structure. The most important of these principles was that faith without good works was meaningless. That central belief led Grandfather to first accept the "doctrine of stewardship" for his great fortune and then to broaden it by creating the great philanthropies later in life. (p. 7)

Beyond Charity: A Century of Philanthropic Innovation
by Eric John Abrahamson, Ph.D.

Rockefeller's interest in the welfare of African Americans at an early stage in his philanthropy was no doubt strengthened by his marriage to Laura Celestia Spelman in 1864. "Cettie," as her friends called her, had grown up in a deeply religious Congregationalist household in Cleveland, where her parents were active abolitionists and supporters of the Underground Railroad. She was an early supporter of the temperance movement as well. (p. 41)

Junior, born on January 29, 1874, shared many of his father's traits but also was profoundly influenced by his mother's homeschooling. As the only son among four children who survived infancy, Junior learned from his mother the spirit and precepts of the New Testament. The family prayed, read the Bible, and recited verses on a daily basis. Every Friday night they attended prayer meeting. They respected Sunday as a day of rest and devotion. (p. 45)

Senior and Junior were both moved to philanthropy by religious views derived from the Puritan traditions of New England. In the Puritan view the faithful were bound to one another by God's love. Charity was a manifestation of that love. (p. 47)

High status or wealth, however, did not

accrue to the individual, but to "the glory of his Creator and the common good of the creature, man." Thus the wealthy and powerful were seen by the community and should be seen by themselves as God's stewards. (p. 47)

Junior was profoundly influenced by his parents' faith as well as the crisis of Protestantism in the late nineteenth century that was prompted by the second scientific and industrial revolution. In the context of the challenge raised by Darwin and others, believers sought to reconcile the Bible with the understandings of science. (p. 48)

Like their Puritan forefathers, Senior and Junior worked assiduously to turn their high ideals into ordinary realities. Both men subscribed to the Puritan notion of two callings: one to a godly life and the other to a specific vocation. For Junior, especially, that vocation was philanthropy. (p. 48)

Born in 1853, Gates was the son of a New York Baptist preacher. At age fifteen, he had become a schoolteacher to help his family pay its bills. Gates confessed to being repulsed by the repressive Puritan faith of his parents when he was a boy. Yet, for Gates, like Rockefeller, this Puritan heritage would have a profound influence on his view of the world. Graduating from the Rochester Theological Seminary, a Baptist institution, Gates moved to Minneapolis to become a pastor at the Fifth Avenue Baptist Church. (p. 56-57)

Gates met George Pillsbury, the flour magnate, and got his first taste of advising the wealthy on their philanthropy when Pillsbury came to him regarding a bequest he intended to make to support a Baptist academy in Minnesota. In 1888, Gates was picked to lead the American Baptist Education Society, with a primary goal of developing a great university in Chicago. (p. 57)

Andrew Carnegie (1835-1919)

My Own Story
by Andrew Carnegie

My power to memorize must have been greatly strengthened by the mode of teaching adopted by my uncle. I cannot name a more important means of benefiting young people than encouraging them to commit favorite pieces to memory and recite them often. One of the trials of my boy's life at school in Dunfermline was committing to memory two double verses of the Psalms which I had to recite daily. My plan was not to look at the Psalm until I had started for school. It was not more than five or six minutes' slow walk, but I could readily master the task in that time, and, as the Psalm was the first lesson, I was prepared and passed through the ordeal successfully. (p. 9)

Triumphant Democracy
by Andrew Carnegie

At the time of the Revolution (1776) there were one thousand four-hundred and sixty-one ministers and one thousand nine-hundred and fifty-one churches, which gave one minister for every two thousand and fifty three souls and a church for every one thousand five hundred and thirty-eight. In 1880 there was a minister for every six-hundred and sixty and a church for every five hundred and fifty-three. Wherever the American settles he begins at once the erection of his schoolhouse and his church. (p. 157-158)

The evils of the State Church flow from its parent, the Monarchy, of which it is the legitimate offspring. Its archbishops and bishops residing in palaces and rolling in wealth are the religious aristocracy; the thousands of poor curates who drag out existence upon pittances represent the masses. The revenues of the State Church exceed five million pounds sterling. The Church owns all kinds of property and is squeamish about none. (p. 161)

Without Church-rate or tithe, without State endowment or state supervision, religion in America has spontaneously acquired a strength which no political support could have given it. It is a living force entering into the lives of the people and drawing them closer together in unity of feeling, and working silently and without sign of the friction which in the mother country results from a union with the State, which, as we have seen, tends strongly to keep the people divided one from another. The power of the church in America change must not be sought, as Burke said of an ideal aristocracy, "in rotten parchments, under dripping and perishing walls, but in full vigor, and acting with vital energy and power, in the character of the leading men and natural interests of the country." Even if judged by the church accommodation provided and the sums spent upon church organizations, Democracy can safely claim that of all the divisions of the English-speaking people, it has produced the most religious community yet known. (p. 164)

Andrew Carnegie: The Man and His Work
by Barnard Alderson

He [Carnegie] describes the parson to suit him to be one who says little and does much. He has, however, very great faith in the refining and elevating influence of music, which he speaks of as heaven's chief medium. (p. 104)

Rich men, he says, have cause to be thankful for one inestimable boon- "they have in their power, during their lives, to busy themselves in organizing benefactions from which the masses of their fellows will derive lasting benefit, and thus they will dignify their own lives." (p. 139)

Mr. Carnegie thinks this new era in the world's history has already dawned; and as the light becomes more distinct he prophecies that the voice of the people will strongly condemn the man who hoards wealth instead of wisely allotting it to better his fellow man. Making handsome bequests before the last hour will not earn the full reward. Giving during his life, in his opinion, the only just and proper course. (p. 142)

Mr. Carnegie has given his gospel the best possible christening, and there are significant signs that he is likely to have many worthy followers. While millions are a burden to some men, and crush both soul and energy, he finds in them no source of anxiety. They are his, and yet they are not. Their disbursement will give him the greatest happiness and abolish all thoughts of anxiety from his mind. (p. 141)

In the course of the article Mr. Carnegie dealt with the seven objects which, in his opinion, were worthy of the attention of those possessed of wealth.

1. To found or enlarge a university.
2. The erection of free libraries.
3. Establishment of hospitals or laboratories.
4. To present public parks.
5. To open public halls with organs.
6. To start swimming baths.
7. To build churches. (p. 145)

Churches as fields for surplus wealth have purposely been reserved until the last, because these being sectarian, every man will be governed by his own attachments; therefore it may be said gifts to churches are not in one sense gifts to the community at large, but to special classes. The millionaire should not figure how cheaply this structure can be built, but how perfect it can be made. But, having given the building, the donor should stop there; the support of the church should be upon its own people. There is not much genuine religion in the congregation or much good to flow from the church which is not supported at home. (p. 147)

Mr. Carnegie concluded his article on "The Best Fields of Philanthropy" with the following impressive declaration: "The Gospel of Wealth but echoes Christ's words; it calls upon the millionaire to sell all he hath and give the highest and the best to the poor, by administering his estate for his fellow men before he is called to lie down and rest upon the bosom of mother earth. So doing he will approach his end no longer the ignoble hoarder of useless millions; poor, very poor indeed in money, but rich, very rich in the affection, gratitude and admiration of his fellow men, and sweeter far, soothed and sustained by the still sweet voice within, which whispering tells him that because he has lived perhaps one small portion of the great world has bettered just a little. This much is sure, against such riches as these no bar will be found at the gates of Paradise." (p. 149)

Specialization began the root of individualism. Then came exchange of products, but after a time barter ceased, and certain articles—wampum, beads, skins, shells—became "money," in which were invested the savings of men. Then was slowly developed, in due progress of time, that beneficiate gospel, "as a man soweth, so shall he reap" (Galatians 6:7)—reward according to service. Many things hitherto held in common became private property. And at last, out of the savings of men (capital), durable things were built, and civilization dawned. Even in our own time not a ton nor a yard of anything can be produced, not a ship nor railroad, not a house, school, university, nor a church built without drawing upon stored-up capital, which is wealth. (p. 13)

The writer lived his early years among workmen and his later years as an employer of labor, and it is incomprehensible to him how any informed man, having at heart the elevation of manual laboring men, could fail to place upon the habit of thrift the highest value, second only to that of temperance, without which no honorable career is possible, for against intemperance no combination of good qualities can prevail. Temperance and thrift are virtues which act and react upon each other, strengthening both, and are seldom found apart. (p. 99)

This is our God-like mission, that every individual in his day and generation push on this march upward, so that each succeeding generation may be better than the preceding. Not one of us can feel his duty done, unless he can say as he approaches his end, that, because he has lived some fellow creature, or some little spot on earth or something upon it, has been made just a little better. (p. 154)

[A Carnegie Anthology](#)
by Margaret B. Wilson

When my country calls for assistance of any kind, I consider it my glorious duty to answer that call. And if the present President should command me to do anything for my country, I should regard it the same as I would the voice of God. (p. 2)

The writer, when traveling round the world, saw nothing that saddened him more than the rival sects of Christians, engaged in proclaiming their respective differences, trying to convert the heathen to a revelation about which they could not agree themselves even so far as to unite in worshipping the same God in the same temple, each sect building its own. (p. 5)

Religion is the highest expression of which a people is capable. There is no reason why we should not try to prepare a people for a better one, but note this, they must be prepared. To force new religions upon anyone is a sad mistake. (p. 9)

In the happiest and holiest homes of today, it is not the man who leads the wife upward, but the infinitely purer and more angelic wife whom the husband reverently follows upon the heavenly path as the highest embodiment of all virtues that have been revealed to him: he for God in her. Throughout the English-speaking race as a rule today, it is the wife and mother who sanctifies the home. (p. 27)

The greatest force is no longer that of brutal war which sows the seeds of future wars, but the supreme force of gentleness and generosity—the golden rule. (p. 70)

What the cross is to the Christian the idol is to the other, and it is nothing more. The worship of both is the Unknown beyond. (p. 76)

Still there is a wide providence for faith. If it does not exactly remove mountains nowadays, it at least enables us to tunnel them, which is much the same thing as far as practical results are concerned. (p. 78)

Two women, my mother and my wife, have made me all that I am. (p. 78)

Theological minds may see in the music suggested an unworthy intruder in domains sacred to dogma; but they should remember that the Bible tells us that in heaven music is the principal source of happiness—the sermon seems nowhere—and it may go hard with such as fail to give it the first place on earth. (p. 136)

The reverend gentleman said that in an ideal Christian community a millionaire would be an impossibility, to which I took the liberty of saying in reply that it was a far guess ahead just what would exist in an ideal community; but one thing was certain, that at least no preacher would be required. (p. 157)

The aspiration of a people for the God-given right to govern themselves is rarely quenched. (p. 170)

Miscellaneous Writings of Andrew Carnegie by Burton J. Hendrick

The millionaire as such has, then, a right to his place in the world, and has no occasion to be ashamed: thus far he serves God in his time and place. (p. 134-135)

It is a growing belief with me that in the not distant future increasing importance will be attached to one truth until it overshadows all others and proves the center around which the religious sentiments will finally gather—the declaration of Christ, "The Kingdom of Heaven is within you." This was the first of several truths inscribed upon the frieze of my library in New York many years ago; there they remain and on the library frieze at Skibo there they shall be inscribed. (p. 316)

Perhaps you will see and suggest that the best test of fitness for a heavenly life hereafter and the strongest assurance of one, is that they have developed the elements of such a life here upon earth, and that unless in some degree the Kingdom of Heaven is within him here, man hopes in vain for heaven beyond. (p. 316-317)

So believing, he stands awe-stricken in the holy presence of the Eternal which makes for righteousness, fearing nothing, asking nothing and, grateful for the manifold blessings already received, he reverently bows his head and murmurs his only prayer, one of self-effacement and resignation "Thy will be done." (p. 319)

John Pierpont Morgan (1837-1913)

J. Pierpont Morgan
by Herbert L. Satterlee

1883
Although he was so busy during this year, he had joined the New York Yacht Club and began to take an active interest in its affairs.

He also became a member of a committee to establish libraries and reading rooms for the use of workingmen in various parts of the city. He was unremitting in his attention to the affairs of St. George's Church and was still on the lookout for a new rector. Finally, he met William S. Rainsford, a young clergyman who had made a pronounced success in Toronto as a revivalist. Rainsford was forceful and fearless, with a most attractive personality, and had become very popular as a preacher. This first meeting, late in the autumn of 1882, resulted in Pierpont's asking Mr. Rainsford to consider coming to St. George's Church and he outlined his program for organizing the affairs of the church. He also told Mr. Rainsford that as rector he would have a free hand in running the church, and that he, Pierpont, would find the money to carry out the plans to which they had agreed. (p. 210)

1883
It was with great satisfaction that he had Mr. Johnson install a complete electric light equipment in the rectory of St. George's Church for his friend Dr. Rainsford, and also in the church gymnasium which was much used by the young men and boys of the congregation. (p. 215)

1886
On April 3, he was elected a member of the Board of Trustees of the Cathedral of St. John the Divine, and at once took an active part in raising money for the Building Fund. However, he continued to give a great deal of time to the affairs of St. George's Church, and enthusiastically backed up Dr. Rainsford in his many enterprises to help the people of the East Side in their daily lives. (p. 236)

1889
In October, Pierpont sat as a delegate in the Triennial Convention of the Episcopal Church, which was held that year in St. George's on Stuyvesant Square. He had given a great deal of time to the preparation for this gathering, making arrangements for the seating of the delegates in the church, giving them daily lunch during the three weeks' session and lodging and entertaining them. Moreover, his committee on the revision of the Prayer Book made its report. (p. 251)

1890
During the preceding winter Mr. Morgan had become interested in Dr. Rainsford's idea of providing a place out of town where women and children could go for relief from the city's heat during the summer months. This spring he bought and presented to the church a plot in Rockaway Park Long Island; and on this St. George's "Cottage-by the-Sea" was built. It was designed so that about fifty mothers and babies could spend a week or two there, with ample dressing rooms for bathers who came down for the day. John Reichert and his wife were put in charge, and it has been a godsend to many a poor woman who otherwise could not have got out of the city with her children in the hot season. (p. 255)

1901
On Christmas morning he and all his family were at St. George's Church as usual. There was a great crowd, as the Christmas Carols were sung and Dr. Rainsford was at the height

of his popularity as a preacher. After the service Mr. Morgan called on intimate friends to wish them a Merry Christmas and, of course, went in for a few minutes to see the presents at the Hamiltons' and the Satterlees'. (p. 367-368)

1902
The house included not only living quarters for the deaconesses and the consultation and conference rooms, but rooms where women and girls who were tired could find rest and refreshment and other rooms where convalescents who had been discharged from a hospital could get back their strength before returning to work. It goes without saying that the house was of great usefulness in the parish. The building cost Mr. Morgan about $100,000. No one remembers how much he paid for the two lots. (p. 375)

1905
In September Mr. Morgan completed plans for establishing the trade-school of St. George's Church in permanent quarters. Dr. Rainsford had long felt that the best way to keep boys off the street and out of mischief was to keep them busy and years before he had started a trade-school in temporary quarters...For years the school was operated with great success. (p. 426)

[The Great Pierpont Morgan](#)
by Frederick Lewis Allen

Along with thrift went godliness: church attendance twice on Sundays, family hymn-singing Sunday evenings, and the building of a robust religious faith, which was destined to stand almost unmodified throughout his life.

Long afterward Morgan's friend, Dr. William S. Rainsford, the rector of St. George's Church in New York, wrote that Morgan's faith was like a "precious heirloom"- "talent to be wrapped in its own napkin and venerated in the secret place of his soul...in safe disuse." (p. 12)

The first thing Morgan ever collected in his youth, aside from stamps, was the autographs of the Episcopal Bishops. He went on to become not only a formidably successful banker, but a tireless vestryman and church warden, a giver of parish houses and cathedral chapels, an energetic attender of triennial Episcopal Conventions. (p. 13)

The nature and manner of his giving followed a highly personal pattern. In the first place, many of his gifts went quite unpublicized. (You may recall his setting up a trust fund for Dr. Rainsford and telling him to mention it only to Mrs. Rainsford.) None of them involved naming a building for him. Morgan felt that a gentleman should not advertise his benefactions. The chief reason why it is so difficult for a biographer to estimate whether the total of Morgan's gifts was near five million or ten million was that so many of them were made so quietly. (p. 149)

When in the skeptical year 1913 he died, and his will was made public, those who had known him only by reputation gasped at the way in which the document began; how on earth could this monarch of Wall Street, this worldly yachtsman, this lordly spender of millions, have written those tremendous introductory words?—"I commit my soul into the hands of my Savior, in full confidence that having redeemed it and washed it in his most precious blood He will present it faultless before my Heavenly Father; and I entreat my children to maintain and defend, at all hazard and at any cost of personal sacrifice, the blessed doctrine of the complete atonement for sin through the blood of Jesus Christ, once offered, and through that alone. (p. 13)

Henry Ford (1863-1947)

My Philosophy of Industry
by Henry Ford

We should never be fearful of the cost of the right thing. (p. 29)

There was a word once spoken which throws light on this: "Seek ye first the kingdom of God and His righteousness and all these things shall be added unto you." This is from the Sermon on the Mount. It sounds religious but it is just a plain statement of facts. It means just what it says—the reign, the rule, the law of the highest relations. Get that right way, work by that, and you have the world—a world without poverty, without injustice, without need. (p. 38)

The two great hindrances to success are fear and pride. (p. 81)

People who can see the signs of the times begin their own reformation. Charity is no substitute for reform. Poverty is not cured by charity; it is only relieved. Nothing does more to abolish poverty than work. It is not the men who are doing the talking who are solving our problems, but the men who are at work. Idleness warps the mind. (p. 104-105)

Henry Ford: An Interpretation
by Samuel S. Marquis

I have known Henry Ford for twenty years. For a time he was my parishioner, and then for a time I was his employee. (p. 4)

I once preached a sermon for Henry Ford's special benefit. I told him I was going to do so and asked him to be present and hear it. He came. He listened very attentively. He went away. It was a good sermon, if I do say so myself, but so far as I was ever able to see it never fazed him. (p. 80)

Mrs. Ford does much through the regular channels of the church and charity organizations. To her personal interest and wise guidance, the Ford hospital owes more than the public will ever know. To her generosity the Williams House, a church institution and a temporary home for border-line girls, owes its establishment. There are many who could speak as recipients of her private and individual charity. (p. 86)

But to return to Mr. Ford and the church. Frequently are the questions asked, "Is he a churchman?" "Is he a Christian?" "What are his religious views?" "Is he a religious man?" Mr. Ford was baptized and confirmed in the Episcopal Church. (p. 88)

His father was a vestryman in the little Episcopal church in Dearborn. It was in this church that Mr. Ford was baptized and confirmed. (p. 90)

On Charity

Mr. Ford hates the word charity and all that it stands for. (p. 104)

Mr. Ford has no use for the ordinary channels of charity and philanthropy. Such matters are taken care of by other members of the family. To the Red Cross, the Community Fund, the people destitute on account of sickness or the infirmity of years, and to many charitable institutions Mrs. Ford and Edsel give generously. (p. 104-105)

Over one thousand seven hundred cripples were in the employ of the company at the outbreak of the war. In addition to these, some four or five thousand more men, disabled more or less by disease, and who for that reason, would be rejected by industry, were on its payroll. After the war the company agreed to take a thousand handicapped men as fast as they came out of the hospitals. (p. 111)

He decries charity. He makes no attempt to conceal the fact. He believes that money should be made to work, and that men should work for money. He insists that anything that can't pay it's own way has no right to exist. (p. 117)

The requests for money coming into his own office average, so I have been informed, over six million dollars a month. (p. 105)

Today and Tomorrow
by Henry Ford

It is clear up to them now, as trustees, (conservatives in charge of economic machinery vs. radicals who focus on adversity and criticism) to show what they can do further in the way of making our system foolproof, malice-proof, and greed-proof for the benefit of every person in the land. It is a mere matter of social engineering. It may have the effect of reducing "personal fortunes," but it will not have the effect of reducing working capital. What right has a "personal fortune" to be anything but working capital? The time is here when the commanding law is, "to whom much is given, of him much shall be required." (p. 238)

My Life and Work
by Henry Ford

There are many kinds of knowledge, and it depends on what crowd you happen to be in, or how the fashions of the day happen to run, which kind of knowledge is most respected at the moment. There are fashions in knowledge, just as there are in everything else. When some of us were lads, knowledge used to be limited to the Bible. There were certain men in the neighborhood who knew the Book thoroughly, and they were looked to and respected. Biblical knowledge was highly valued then. But now adays it is doubtful whether deep acquaintance with the Bible would be sufficient to win a man a name for learning. (p. 248)

The genius of the United States of America is Christian in the broadest sense, and its destiny is to remain Christian. This carries no sectarian meaning with it but relates to a basic principle which differs from other principles in that it provides for liberty with morality, and pledges society to a code of relations based on fundamental Christian conceptions of human rights and duties. As for prejudice or hatred against persons, that is neither American nor Christian. Our opposition is only to ideas, false ideas, which are sapping the moral stamina of the people. (p. 251)

Written in 1922
A great many things are going to change. We shall learn to be masters rather than servants of Nature. With all our fancied skill we still depend largely on natural resources and think that they cannot be displaced. We dig coal and ore and cut down trees. We use the coal and ore and they are gone; the trees cannot be replaced within a lifetime. We shall someday harness the heat that is all about us and no longer depend on coal—we may now create heat through electricity generated by water power. We shall improve on that method. As chemistry advances I feel quite certain that a method will be found to transform growing things into substances that will endure better than the metals—we have scarcely touched the uses of cotton. Better wood can be made than is grown. The Spirit of true service will create for us. We have only each of us to do our parts sincerely. Everything is possible…"faith is the substance of things hoped for, the evidence of things not seen." (p. 280-281)

Bibliography

Abrahamson, Eric John, Ph.D. *Beyond Charity: A Century of Philanthropic Innovation*. New York: Rockefeller Foundation Centennial Series, 2013.

Alderson, Barnard. *Andrew Carnegie: The Man and His Work*. New York: Doubleday, Page & Co., 1902.

Allen, Frederick Lewis. *The Great Pierpont Morgan*. New York: Harper & Brothers, 1949.

Arbuthnot, Thomas S. *Heroes of Peace: A History of the Carnegie Hero Fund Commission*. The Carnegie Hero Fund Commission, 1935.

Bridge, James Howard. *Portraits and Personalities in the Frick Galleries*. New York: Aldine Book Company, 1929.

____. *The History of the Carnegie Steel Company*. New York: The Aldine Book Company, 1903.

Bringhurst, Bruce. *Antitrust And The Oil Company: The Standard Oil Cases, 1890-1911*. Westport, Connecticut, London, England: Greenwood Press, 1979.

Bryan, Ford R. *Friends Families & Forays: Scenes from Life and Times of Henry Ford*. Dearborn, Michigan: Ford Books, 2002.

Butler, Joseph G. Jr. *Fifty Years of Iron and Steel*. Cleveland: The Penton Press, 1920.

Carnegie, Andrew; Helps, Sir Arthur. *How to Win a Fortune. The Transaction of Business*. Madison: Eddy Publishing Company, 1904.

____. *My Own Story*. Boston and New York: The Carnegie Dunfermline Trust, 1920.

____. *Problems of To-Day*. New York: Doubleday, Page & Company, 1908.

____. *The Empire of Business*. New York: Doubleday, Page & Company, 1902.

____. *The Gospel of Wealth*. New York: Double Day, Page & Company, 1900.

____. *The Gospel of Wealth*. Belford: Applewood Books, 1998. (Reprint)

____. *Triumphant Democracy.* New York: Charles Scribner's Sons, 1886.

Carr, Albert Z. *John D. Rockefeller's Secret Weapon*. New York, Toronto, London: McGraw-Hill Book Company, Inc., 1962.

Cecil, William A.V. *Biltmore*. Asheville, The Biltmore Company, 1975.

Chapple, William Dismore. *George Peabody*. Salem: Peabody Museum of Salem, Massachusetts, 1933.

Chernow, Ron. *Titan: The Life of John D. Rockefeller Sr*. New York: Random House, 1998.

Choules, Rev. Charles Overton. *The Cruise of the Steam Yacht North Star*. Boston: Bould and Lincoln, 1854.

Coffin, Henry Sloan. *A Half Century of the Union Theological Seminary 1896-1945*. New York: Charles Scribner's Sons, 1954.

____. *Social Aspects of the Cross*. New York: Hodder & Stoughton, 1911.

____. *The Portraits of Jesus Christ in the New Testament*. New York: The Macmillan Company, 1928.

Conn, Frances G. *Ida Tarbell, Muckraker.* Nashville, New York: Thomas Nelson Inc., 1972.

Croffut, W.A. *The Vanderbilt's and the Story of Their Fortune.* Chicago and New York: Belford, Clarke & Company, 1886.

Deems, Charles F. *The Gospel of Common Sense: As Contained in the Canonical Epistle of James.* New York: Wilbur B. Ketcham, 1888.

Depew, Chauncey M. *My Memories of Eighty Years.* New York: Charles Scribner's Sons, 1922.

Dickson, William B. *History of Carnegie Veteran Association.* Montclair: Mountain Press, 1938.

Ernst, Joseph W. *"Dear Father"/ "Dear Son".* Rockefeller University: Fordham University Press, 1994.

Fay, Charles Norman. *Social Justice: The Moral of the Henry Ford Fortune.* Cambridge, Mass: The Cosmos Press, 1926.

Ford, Henry. *Ford Ideals.* Dearborn: The Dearborn Publishing Company, 1922.

____. *My Life & Work.* London: William Heinemann Ltd., 1924.

____. *My Philosophy of Industry.* New York: Coward-McCann, Inc., 1929.

____. *Today and Tomorrow.* Garden City: Doubleday, Page & Company, 1926.

Fosdick, Raymond B. *American Police Systems.* New York: The Century Co., 1920.

____. *Adventure in Giving.* New York and Evanston: Harper & Row, Publishers, 1962.

____. *Commission on Training Camp Activities.* Washington D.C.: The War Department, 1917.

____. *John D. Rockefeller, Jr.: A Portrait.* New York: Harper and Brothers, 1956.

____. *Letters on the League of Nations.* Princeton, New Jersey: Princeton University Press, 1966.

____. *The Rockefeller Foundation: A Review for 1941.* New York: The Rockefeller Foundation, 1942.

____. *The Story of the Rockefeller Foundation.* New York: Harper and Brothers, 1952.

Gates, Frederick T. *The Truth About Mr. Rockefeller and the Merritts.* New York: Gates, 1911.

Goulder, Grace. *John D. Rockefeller: The Cleveland Years.* Cleveland: The Western Reserve Historical Society, 1972.

Govenar, Alan; Maack, Mary Niles. *Anne Morgan: Photography, Philanthropy, & Advocacy.* New York: The American Friends of Blerancourt, 2016.

Hanaford, Phebe A. *The Life of George Peabody.* Boston: B. B. Russell, 1870.

Hendrick, Burton J. *Miscellaneous Writings of Andrew Carnegie, V. 2.* Garden City: Doubleday, Doran & Company, Inc., 1933.

____, *The Life of Andrew Carnegie V.1&2.* Garden City: Doubleday, Doran & Company, Inc., 1932.

Henderson, Daniel. *Louise Whitfield Carnegie: The Life of Mrs. Andrew Carnegie.* New York 22: Hastings House, 1950.

Hovey, Carl. *The Life Story of J. Pierpont Morgan.* London: William Heinemann, 1912.

Interchurch World Movement of North America. *World Survey.* New York City: Interchurch Press, 1920.

Johnson, Willis Fletcher. *History of the Johnstown Flood.* Boston: Edgewood Publishing Co., 1889.

Josephson, Matthew. *The Robber Barons: The Great American Capitalists 1861-1901.* Norwalk, Connecticut: The Easton Press, 1987.

Kert, Bernice. *Abby Aldrich Rockefeller: The Women in the Family.* New York: Random House, 1993.

Lane, Wheaton J. *Commodore Vanderbilt: An Epic of the Steam Age.* New York: Alfred A. Knopf, 1942.

Loebl, Suzanne. *America's Medics: The Rockefellers and Their Astonishing Cultural Legacy.* New York: Harper Collins Publishers, 2010.

MacDowell, Dorothy Kelly. *Commodore Vanderbilt and His Family.* Hendersonville, NC: Dorothy K. MacDowell, 1989.

Marquis, Samuel S. *Henry Ford: An Interpretation.* Boston: Little Brown, and Company, 1923.

Miller, James Martin. *The Real Story of Henry Ford.* United Kingdom of Great Britain and Colonies, 1922.

Montague, Gilbert Holland. *The Rise and Progress of the Standard Oil Company.* New York and London: Harper & Brothers Publishers, 1904.

Moody, John. *The Truth About Trusts.* New York: Moody Publishing Company, 1904.

Moore, Samuel Taylor; Pound, Arthur. *They Told Barron.* New York and London: Harper & Brothers Publishers, 1930.

____. *The More They Told Barron.* New York and London: Harper & Brothers Publishers, 1931.

Nevins, Allan. *John D. Rockefeller: The Heroic Age of American Enterprise V.1 & 2.* New York: Charles Scribner's Sons, 1940.

____. *Study in Power: John D. Rockefeller, Industrialist, Philanthropist V.1 & 2.* New York, London: Charles Scribner's Sons, 1953.

Painter, Patricia Scollard. *Henry Ford Hospital.* Detroit, Michigan: Henry Ford Health System, 1997.

Peyser, Ethel. *The House That Music Built: Carnegie Hall.* New York: Robert M. Mc Bride & Company, 1936.

Philadelphia Engineering Works, Limited. Chicago: Western Office, 1893.

Rainsford, William. *The Land of the Lion.* New York: Doubleday, Page & Company, 1909.

Rockefeller, David. *Creative Management in Banking.* New York, San Francisco, Toronto, London: McGraw-Hill Book Company, 1964.

____. *David Rockefeller: Memoirs.* New York: Random House, 2002.

Rockefeller, John D. *Random Reminiscences of Men and Events.* London: William Heinemann, 1909.

____. *Random Reminiscences of Men and Events.* Lawrence Rockefeller, Editor. Terrytown: Sleepy Hollow Press, 1984. (Reprint)

Rockefeller Jr., John D. *The Colorado Industrial Plan.* New York: Atlantic Monthly, 1916.

____. *The Last Rivet.* New York: Columbia University Press, 1940.

____. *The Personal Relation in Industry*. New York: Boni and Liveright Publishers, 1924.

Ruminski, Dan; Dutka, Alan. *Cleveland in the Gilded Age*. Charleston, South Carolina: History Press, 2013.

Satterlee, Herbert L. J. *Pierpont Morgan*. New York: The MacMillan Company, 1939.

____. *The Life of John Pierpont Morgan*. New York: Privately Printed, 1937.

Savage, Howard J. *Fruit of an Impulse*. New York: Harcourt, Bruce and Company, 1953.

Schwab, Charles M. *Succeeding With What You Have*. New York: The Century Company, 1917.

Shaplen, Robert. *Toward the Well-Being of Mankind*. London: Hutchinson, 1964.

Simonds, William A. *Henry Ford: His Life, His Work, His Genius*. Indianapolis, New York: The Bobbs-Merrill Company, 1943.

Smith, Arthur D. Howden. *Commodore Vanderbilt: An Epic American Achievement*. New York: Robert M. McBride & Company, 1927.

Stanley, Arthur Penrhyn. *Addresses and Sermons in America*. New York: Macmillan & Co., 1879.

Stidger, William L. *Henry Ford: The Man and His Motives*. New York: George H. Doran Company, No Date.

Stories of Noble Lives. Story of Cyrus Field: The Projector of the Atlantic Telegraph. London: T. Nelson and Sons, Paternoster Row, 1878.

Taft, William Howard. *Anti-Trust Act and the Supreme Court*. New York and London: Harper and Brothers Publishers, 1914.

Tarbell, Ida M. *All in the Day's Work*. New York: The Macmillan Company, 1939.

____. *The History of the Standard Oil Company, V1&2*. New York: McClure, Phillips & Co., 1905.

____. *The History of the Standard Oil Company*. New York: Peter Smith, 1950.

____. *The Life of Elbert H. Gary: A Story of Steel*. New York, London: D. Appleton and Company, 1926.

The Carnegie Endowment for International Peace. *A Manual of Public Benefactions of Andrew Carnegie*. Washington: The Carnegie Endowment for International Peace, 1919.

The Commission of Inquiry, The Interchurch World Movement. *Report on the Steel Strike of 1919*. New York: Harcourt, Brace and Howe, 1920.

The Committee. *This Ministry*. Reinhold Niebuhr, Editor. New York: Charles Scribner's Sons, 1945.

Vanderbilt Jr., Cornelius. *Farewell to Fifth Avenue*. New York: Simon and Schuster, 1935.

Vanderbilt II, Arthur T. *Fortune's Children: The Fall of the House of Vanderbilt*. Norwalk, Connecticut: The Easton Press, 1993.

Wallis, Severn Teackle. *Discourse on the Life and Character of George Peabody*. Annapolis: Order of the General Assembly of Maryland, 1870.

Webster, E. Lucile. *An Autobiography of a One-Room School Teacher*. Dearborn: E. Lucile Webster, 1978.

Whittles, Thomas D. *Frank Higgins Trail Blazer*. New York: Interchurch Press, 1920.

Wilgus, Horace L. *A Study of the United States Steel Corporation*. Chicago: Callaghan & Company, 1901.

Wilson, Margaret B. *A Carnegie Anthology*. New York: Privately Printed, 1915.

Winkler, John K. *John D. A Portrait in Oils*. New York: The Vanguard Press, 1929.

_____. *Morgan the Magnificent: The Life of J. Pierpont Morgan*. Garden City: Garden City Publishing Co., Inc., 1930.

Wilson, Philip Whitwell. *George Peabody Esq.: An Interpretation*. Bruce R. Payne, 1926.

The Men Who Built America. Lionsgate History.com, 2012.

Acknowledgements

This study would not have come into being without the early contribution from our late friend, Peb Jackson, who gave us wise counsel and good advice.

Our friends at Scottsdale Bible Church helped shape *Transformational Living: Discover Your Kingdom Assignment*, while a special thanks goes to their Stewardship Pastor John Corpstein who spent many hours giving both guidance and encouragement.

We could never say "thank you" enough to the participants throughout the country who attended a pilot presentation of *Transformational Living: Discover Your Kingdom Assignment* then provided helpful feedback and encouragement.

Mission Increase employees worked, often with short notice, to complete a task and further develop *Transformational Living: Discover Your Kingdom Assignment*, and we are grateful to each of them.

We appreciate the team at 610Media who designed, edited, created supplemental content, and guided the publication process.

Finally, we acknowledge both the role of the Holy Spirit and the role of Scripture in *Transformational Living: Discover Your Kingdom Assignment*.

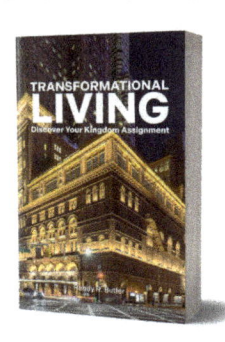

Read the book on which this series is based. *Transformational Living: Discover Your Kingdom Assignment* by Randy R. Butler

Available now online through Amazon, Walmart, Target, Books-A-Million or wherever you buy books!

For bulk orders and group study bundles, visit missionincrease.org/transformational-living or scan the QR code above.

Printed in the USA
CPSIA information can be obtained
at www.ICGtesting.com
LVHW071532010924
789765LV00001B/3